The Water Walker

written and illustrated by
Joanne Robertson

Second Story Press

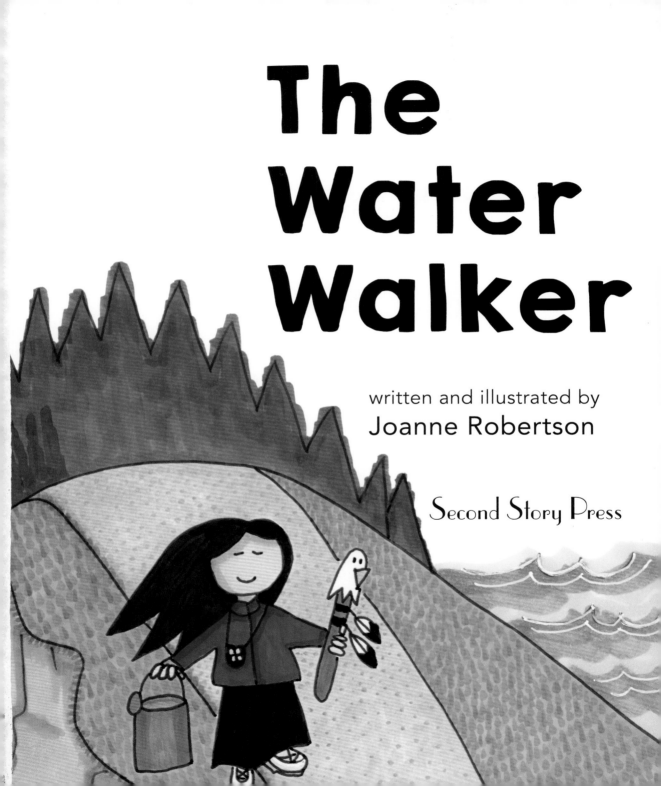

Nokomis loved Nibi,

and Nibi loved
Nokomis.

Rain

or shine,

hot

or cold,

calm

or wild.

Every morning, like the women in her
family before her, Nokomis hopped out of
bed, and before doing anything else, she sang.
"Gichi miigwech, Nibi, for the life you give
to every living thing on Earth. I love you.
I respect you."

But one day a wise ogimaa told her,
"In my lifetime, the day will come
when an ounce of water costs more
than an ounce of gold.
What are you going to do about it?"

Like an arrow, his words pierced Nokomis's heart.

She looked around.
She saw how people
were disrespecting
the water, wasting it,
making it unfit for life.

Day turned to night,
nights turned to weeks,
and Nokomis remembered
the ogimaa's words.

A few moons went by,
and then one night,
Nokomis had a bawaajgan.

Early next morning, Nokomis called her sister and kwewok niichiis over for tea to talk about their responsibility to protect Nibi.

Four days later, Nokomis
and the Mother Earth Water
Walkers, as they came to be
known, found themselves
standing on the side of the road…
wearing sneakers. Nokomis
carried a copper pail full of Nibi
in one hand and a Migizi Staff
in the other.

If no one noticed Nibi, maybe they would notice the Water Walkers. Maybe someone would ask why they carried Nibi in their copper pail. Maybe someone would be moved to protect Nibi too.

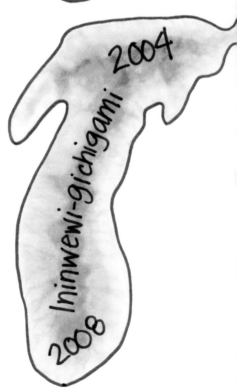

Nokomis and the Mother Earth Water Walkers walked around all the Great Lakes and the St. Lawrence River. They walked every spring for seven years.

Anishinaabewi – gichigami
2003

Ininwewi-gichigami
2004
2008

They prayed and sang to Nibi.
They left semaa in every lake, river,
stream, and puddle they met.

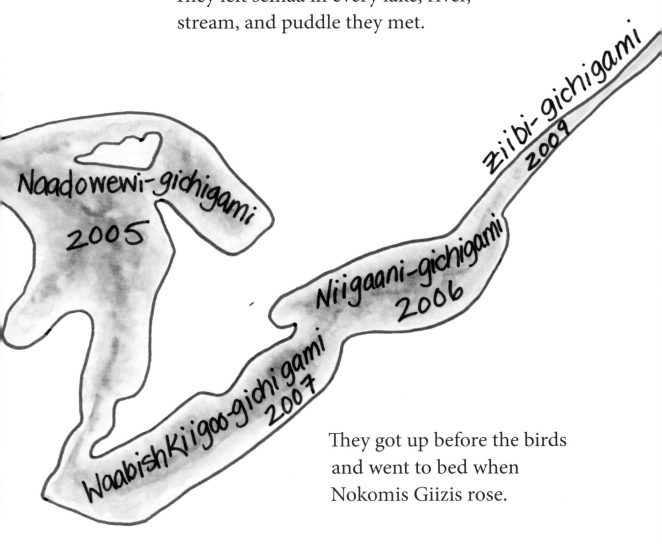

Naadowewi-gichigami
2005

Ziibi-gichigami
2009

Niigaani-gichigami
2006

Waabishkiigoo-gichigami
2007

They got up before the birds
and went to bed when
Nokomis Giizis rose.

Nokomis was interviewed on television, in newspapers, and on radio. She was even in movies. But big companies, politicians, and even her next door neighbors, still did not feel the urgency to protect Nibi.

"What more can I do?" wondered Nokomis.

A year later, over by the Atlantic Ocean, a niichii-kwe had a bawaajgan, which she shared with Nokomis as soon as she woke up.

Nokomis shared the bawaajgan with all the people she had met during her previous walks. Word spread fast across Turtle Island. Everyone began to prepare.

Next thing you know, there were kwewok standing at each salt Nibi surrounding Turtle Island, with a copper pail in one hand and a Migizi Staff in the other...

wearing sneakers.

In the west, Nokomis and the Mother Earth Water Walkers set off from the Pacific Ocean saying, "Nga-zhichige Nibi onji. I will do it for the water."

One year after a devastating oil spill, Nokomis and the Water Walkers set off from the Gulf of Mexico singing to Nibi and praying for healing for Nibi.

Next, Nokomis and the Water Walkers set off from the Atlantic Ocean in the east. At the sendoff, they walked barefoot on the rocks and the beautiful petroglyphs and sang to Nibi.

Machias

Putting on their sneakers, they started out on the migration trail their ancestors traveled hundreds of years before.

In the frigid north, the ice was five feet thick. Nokomis and the Mother Earth Water Walkers put semaa on the frozen Nibi, singing their thanks, respect, and love.

Saltwater tears filled the Mother Earth Water Walkers' eyes, as the four salt Nibi met Lake Superior.

"One day the four salt Nibi will be reborn as clouds
and be carried home on the wind," said Nokomis.

Nokomis went through three knees
and eleven pairs of sneakers
walking for Nibi.

She got her knees replaced and is
at home resting up, taking the time
to surf online for new sneakers.

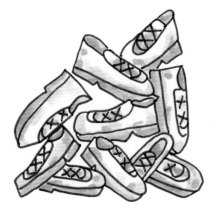

Every morning she puts down her semaa for Nibi and sings her gratitude. She prays people wake up and realize that without Nibi there is no life....

And she continues to wonder...

"What are you
going to do about it?"

Ojibwe words and their pronunciations

kwe (*quay*) - woman

kwewok (*quay-wuk*) - women

bawaajgan (*buh-wawj-gun*) - dream

niichii (*knee-chee*) - friend

gichi miigwech (*gih-chih mee-gwetch*) - thank you very much

nokomis (*no-kuh-miss*) - grandmother

jiimaan (*jee-mawn*) - canoe, boat

migizi *(mih-gih-zee)* - bald eagle

Nokomis Giizis *(no-kuh-miss ghee-ziss)* - moon

ogimaa *(oh-gih-maw)* - leader, chief

semaa *(say-maw)* - sacred tobacco

Turtle Island - North America

Nibi *(nih-bih)* - water

Nokomis Josephine Mandamin is from Wikwemikong on Manitoulin Island and now resides in Thunder Bay, Ontario in Canada.

On a rainy day in April 2003, Nokomis and the Mother Earth Water Walkers set out on their first walk for water. Nokomis was inspired to act by the prophecy Midewiwin Grand Chief Eddie Benton-Banai shared, warning that water would become scarce and expensive if we didn't reverse our carelessness.

Nokomis has walked in all kinds of weather, on the sides of highways, down gravel paths, and even up mountains. No matter how sore and tired she was, she continued to walk and sing to the water. By doing this she teaches us that we must learn to flow like a river because healthy water moves freely.

Nokomis walks for all life on Earth…trees, birds, plants, insects, animals, your family, and all of your grandchildren's grandchildren yet to come. Nokomis asks us to think about this and make decisions based on this knowledge.

Nokomis Josephine Mandamin is as precious as the water! During her 2015 walk alone, she put almost 4,500,000 footsteps on her sneakers! Next time you're at the mall or out walking your dog, count your footsteps. She sacrifices weeks sometimes months away from her home every year to pray and sing for the water. She hopes that some of you reading this book will be inspired to help her protect it.

You can learn more about her walks at www.motherearthwaterwalk.com.

If you want to share with her what you are doing to protect the water, you may mail your letters to:

Nokomis Josephine Mandamin
628 Harold Street North
Thunder Bay, Ontario
Canada
P7C 4E3

Josephine (left) with Joanne Robertson

Nibi, Biidaasige, Bawdwaywidun,
The Water Walkers, H.B.
—J.R.

_____

Library and Archives Canada Cataloguing in Publication

Robertson, Joanne, 1960-, author
The water walker / by Joanne Robertson.

ISBN 978-1-77260-038-4 (hardcover)

1. Traditional ecological knowledge—Great Lakes Region (North America)—
Juvenile literature. 2. Human ecology—Great Lakes Region (North America)—
Juvenile literature. 3. Native peoples—Ecology—Canada—Juvenile literature.
4. Water conservation—Great Lakes Region (North America)—Juvenile literature.
5. Environmental protection—Great Lakes Region (North America)—Juvenile literature.
6. Ojibwa Indians—Science—Canada—Juvenile literature. I. Title.

E78.G7R63 2017   j304.209713   C2017-902646-1

Second Story Press gratefully acknowledges the support
of the Ontario Arts Council and the Canada Council for the Arts for
our publishing program. We acknowledge the financial support of the
Government of Canada through the Canada Book Fund.

ONTARIO ARTS COUNCIL
CONSEIL DES ARTS DE L'ONTARIO
an Ontario government agency
un organisme du gouvernement de l'Ontario

Canada Council   Conseil des Arts
for the Arts   du Canada

Funded by the Government of Canada
Financé par le gouvernement du Canada

Canadä

MIX
Paper from
responsible sources
FSC® C124385

Published by
Second Story Press
20 Maud Street, Suite 401
Toronto, Ontario, Canada
M5V 2M5
www.secondstorypress.ca